Health, & Healing

A CHRISTIAN PERSPECTIVE

Published by
SAINT ANDREW PRESS
on behalf of the
CHURCH of SCOTLAND
BOARD of SOCIAL RESPONSIBILITY
Charis House, 47 Milton Road East
Edinburgh EH15 2SR

Telephone: 0131 657 2000
Fax: 0131 657 5000
E-mail: info@charis.org.uk

Contents

Preface by Rev. David Lunan   iii

Introduction by Ann Allen   iv

HEALTH & HEALING – A Christian Perspective

▼   BIBLICAL and THEOLOGICAL EXPOSITION   4

▼   RESOURCES for the HEALING MINISTRY   15

▼   A LETTER to SOMEONE
    embarking on a HEALING MINISTRY   17

▼   FURTHER READING   21

▼   DISCUSSION QUESTIONS on HEALTH and HEALING   22

▼   OTHER PUBLICATIONS from
    the BOARD OF SOCIAL RESPONSIBILITY   26

▼   The CHURCH of SCOTLAND
    BOARD of SOCIAL RESPONSIBILITY   28

General Editors: Hugh Brown
and Kristine Gibbs.
Design concept: Mark Blackadder.
Photograph: © Image Bank, illustration by
Christa Keiffer.
Typeset in Palatino and Helvetica.

First **published** in 1998 on behalf of:
CHURCH of SCOTLAND
BOARD of SOCIAL RESPONSIBILITY
by SAINT ANDREW PRESS
121 George Street, Edinburgh EH2 4YN

Copyright ©
CHURCH of SCOTLAND
BOARD of SOCIAL RESPONSIBILITY 1998

British Library in Cataloguing Data
A catalogue record for this book is
available from the British Library.

ISBN 0 86153 269 4

Printed and **bound** in Scotland by:
Hugh K Clarkson & Sons Ltd,
West Calder.

Preface

HARRY Emerson Fosdick observes that if God wants something done, people must co-operate by *working* (to put bricks on top of one another, to till the soil); or by *thinking* (to discover a cure for cancer, to work out the wisest way to act); or by *praying*. Some things only happen when people pray, and we have to learn to pray. Indeed prayer – meaning an expression of our relationship with a loving God – is our unique contribution to any situation. People with no faith can be every bit as kind and thoughtful and active and patient as people with faith and sometimes even more so – it's just that we know we need prayer.

Healing is one of the many things about which we pray, but healing is central to all our work and worship. It is worth asking about any activity or organisation within the Church, "Who is being healed by this?" From being reconciled to God to restoring broken relationships, from praying for someone in hospital to establishing a healthy society, from seeking a wholesome, holy, lifestyle, to the healing of the nations – everything we do as followers of Christ should bring healing somewhere to someone. The Church is God's instrument of healing in the world, and the privilege is, broken and wounded though we be, to be a part of it. There is grace.

I hope that the publishing of this report, and the discussions and prayers it provokes, will help us as individuals, and as the body of Christ, to be challenged and inspired to obey the Great Physician, not only in preaching the gospel, but in healing the sick.

Rev. David Lunan
Study Group on Health and Healing

Introduction

THERE is a generally accepted view that we are a generation who have never had it so good. We have enjoyed enormous technological and scientific developments, and yet physical, emotional and spiritual health still eludes so many. People, broken and hurting, turn away from standard remedies and desperately seek help in bizarre alternatives and therapies.

The Church's task is to enable folk to become full human beings. We have in Jesus Christ a Lord and master who came to set us free, through and through, so that we can become the whole people God intended us to be: freed from whatever confines us. Freedom can mean different things to different people – being freed from the burdens of physical or spiritual problems, relationship problems or dependency.

This report focuses on Christian healing; the *why*, its biblical foundation; the *where*, its place in the Church; and the *how*, the practical ministry of prayerful healing.

It is an accessible and profound treatment of a much misunderstood area of the Church's mandate.

May it inspire many of us who read it to care and pray more as we love one another in an increasingly loveless world.

Ann Allen
Convener, Board of Social Responsibility
OCTOBER 1998

Health & Healing

A CHRISTIAN PERSPECTIVE

THE General Assembly of 1996, in response to an Overture from the Presbytery of England, resolved to:

> *Instruct the Board of Social Responsibility in pursuance of its remit, in consultation with the Panel on Doctrine, to provide a biblical and theological exposition of the nature and scope of the healing ministry for the guidance of Christian people, and bring forward guidelines for the conduct of services and for pastoral care.*

Background

It may be helpful to recall that the Church of Scotland has already addressed the issues to which the instruction directs us.

In particular, the General Assembly of 1954 appointed a Commission anent Spiritual Healing, and the Commission had as its remit:

> *To investigate the matter of Spiritual Healing, to examine the theological implications, and formulate, with the approval of the General Assembly, definite guidance for both ministers and laymen of the Church.* (1958, p 909)

This Commission issued an Interim Report in 1955 and a final Report in 1958. In turning to these reports, we were struck by their theological depth, allied, as it was, to wise pastoral guidance and counsel. The desire for such a Commission reflected a growing interest in this matter with the Commission suggesting that

> *"the new interest which has arisen both in England and Scotland in recent years in what is sometimes called 'Divine Healing', sometimes 'Spiritual Healing', is to be welcomed .... So far as Scotland is concerned, the movement has been on the whole quiet and informal in its manifestations. But, in about twenty Presbyteries, some kind of healing activities are carried on, ranging from simple prayers for the sick to regular Services of Healing. There are some forty congregational groups in Edinburgh and a similar number in Glasgow; while here and there throughout the country individual ministers are working independently along similar lines."* (1958, p 914)

" ... in the 1950s there was a considerable groundswell of interest in the question of healing."

Thus, we note that in the 1950s there was a considerable groundswell of interest in the question of healing which we might judge to be as great, if not greater, than that which is to be found in the Church of Scotland today.

Thereafter, the General Assembly of 1980 established a Committee on Health and Healing, within the (then) Department of Social Responsibility. This Committee sought

> **"to enable the Church to respond to God's call to a ministry of healing as part of its total ministry, both corporately in its congregational life and individually through its members [and to] express the Church's concern for health and healing in the life of the community, both locally and nationally."**

(General Assembly 1980,
Social Responsibility remit)

Thus, we note that there has already been a sustained period of reflection upon, and promotion of, the healing ministry within the Church through publications and through annual conferences sponsored by the Board. In seeking to fulfil the current instruction, we would not wish to neglect the results of the previous work of this Committee.

Therefore, in the light of what has been previously undertaken, we shall not hesitate to draw upon the theological and pastoral resources already generated by the Commission on Spiritual Healing and the Committee on Health and Healing, and would again commend them to the Church.

> " … we are still very much at the 'pioneering' stage of finding out what it means to be 'the Church as a healing community'."

Nonetheless, there remains a strong sense that we are still very much at the "pioneering" stage of finding out what it means to be "the Church as a healing community", and the challenge "to provide a biblical and theological exposition of the nature and scope of the healing ministry" is one to which there needs to be a renewed response.

A working group from the Board, with representatives from the Panel on Doctrine and the Panel on Worship, was established to respond to this instruction from the General Assembly. The group is greatly indebted to work done by the Rev. Dr John Wilkinson and the Rev. David Lunan in producing this response. The Report is in three sections:

1   a biblical and theological exposition;
2   a guide to available resources;
3   and pastoral guidelines expressed in the form of a letter to someone who senses a call to a healing ministry.

BIBLICAL and THEOLOGICAL EXPOSITION

The Concept of Health

> " ... the most appropriate word in English to sum up the essential nature of health would be 'well-being'."

No understanding of the nature and scope of the healing ministry of the Church can be obtained without some prior discussion of the nature and scope of health and healing, and this paper begins with such a discussion.

The word "health" belongs to a group of words which came to Britain with the Anglo-Saxon invasion of the fifth century AD and first appears in the translation of the Psalms and the Gospels into that language. It is derived from the Teutonic root *hal* ("whole") and gave rise to the words "wholeness", "holiness", "hale", as well as "health". If we were to sum up the essential nature of health in one word in English, the most appropriate one would be "well-being". This was the word used in the constitution of the World Health Organisation (1948) where health was defined as "a state of complete physical, mental and social well-being and not merely the absence of disease or infirmity".[1] In 1984 the World Health Organisation (WHO) invited its members to include a "spiritual dimension" in their health service planning, thus recognising an important aspect of health and health care which the definition had previously omitted.[2]

However, as in the case of the word "health", the term "well-being" needs to be provided with both content and context for it to be

---

1   World Health Organisation, Basic Documents: Constitution (Geneva: WHO, 1948), page 1.
2   WHO Chronicle: Report of the 37th World Health Assembly (Geneva: WHO, 1984), vol 38, page 172 – "Spiritual dimension and TCDC in Health For All".

meaningful. By derivation, "well-being" means "being what you will to be" (the words "well" and "will" are cognate words). Therefore, our understanding of the nature of health and well-being will depend on what we believe about human nature and destiny. For Christians, these words would be understood in the context of the nature and will of God as revealed by His love towards us and the demands of that love upon us. His love desires our complete well-being and to that end he sent his Son to die on the Cross that we might be forgiven and restored to fellowship with Him, the original purpose of our creation.

> " ... our understanding of the nature of health and well-being will depend on what we believe about human nature and destiny."

The Biblical Background

The Bible tells us that human beings were created in "the image and likeness of God" (Genesis 1: 26) and therefore they must have been created healthy since God is healthy in the fullest sense of that term. The human beings which He had created were included in God's verdict when He pronounced all that He had made to be "very good" (Genesis 1: 31). As we read on in the Old Testament, we find that it very rarely uses the word "health", although it soon becomes obvious that it is very much concerned with the health of human beings. Health is not defined so much as described in terms of its characteristics. These are set forth in the lives of people and the demands of God upon them.

Two concepts which most fully enshrine the Old Testament understanding of health are those of *shalom* and *righteousness*. On the one hand, *shalom*, most commonly translated "peace", denotes the presence of wholeness, harmony and well-being in all spheres of life, whether physical, mental or spiritual, social or national.

On the other hand, *righteousness,* used in the context of relationships leads us to define health as a right relationship of a person to God, to themselves, to their neighbour and to their environment. When these relationships are right they find expression in a person's life as uprightness of character and wholeness of being and living.

The Old Testament sees health or lack of it as relating to obedience ("If only you will obey the Lord your God ... then I shall never bring on you any of the sufferings which I brought on the Egyptians; for I the Lord am your healer" – Exodus 15: 26). Health is a right relationship to God and it is through such a relationship that the other human relationships are made right. If any of these break down the result is ill-health, of the individual or the community or both. In the Old Testament the restoration of a right relationship with God was through the sacrificial system set out in the Pentateuch. The restoration of other right relationships followed obedience to those laws of God that regulated life and behaviour – laws of personal, social and environmental hygiene, the observance of which was important in the promotion of health and the prevention of disease.

> "Health is a right relationship to God and it is through such a relationship that the other human relationships are made right."

In the New Testament the central concept of *salvation* is used both in the particular sense of healing as well as referring to the ultimate "rescue" of believers in Jesus Christ. For example, in the incident involving the woman with the haemorrhage (Mark 5: 34) the word *sozo* ("save") is translated in its sentence as, "Your faith has made you well". Again, the great theme of *reconciliation/atonement* signals that health is most fully found in the restoration of relationships, with God in Christ and to each other. The New Testament uses other words to denote health: "blessedness" (Matthew 5: 3-12), "maturity" (Ephesians 4: 13) and "holiness" (1 Thessalonians 5: 23). Jesus summed up the New Testament idea of health when he described it as an overflowing fullness of life (John 10: 10).

However, the New Testament tells us more about healing than about health. The 1958 Report, already referred to, observes:

Any study of the Gospels makes it immediately plain that in the public ministry of Jesus, preaching and healing went hand in hand. At first sight, indeed, it may seem strange that he was prepared to spend so much of his time and strength in the cure of physical and mental illness of all kinds. We read of no case of sickness brought to Him being met with reluctance or refusal to help. "Now when the sun was setting, all they that had any sick with divers diseases brought them unto him, and he laid his hands on every one of them and healed them" *(Luke 4: 40). The reason is that the healing mission of Jesus seems clearly to have been part of His whole redemptive mission. "I am come that men might have life, and that they might have it more abundantly," He declared. Whatever weakens man's [sic] powers, lessens his well-being, or spoils his true happiness, Christ saw as a frustration of God's purpose of love. He had to come to set men free alike from spiritual blindness, from moral servitude, and from physical infirmities; to renew them in body, mind and spirit, so that they should be able to enter into their true destiny as sons of God and citizens of his Kingdom. This redemptive mission of Christ is fulfilled alike in His preaching and teaching and in His healing. "And Jesus went about all Galilee, teaching in their synagogues, and preaching the Gospel of the kingdom, and healing all manner of sickness and all manner of disease among the people" (Matthew 4: 23).*

> "We read of no case of sickness brought to Him being met with reluctance or refusal to help."

Although Jesus' own acts of healing were physical, they were always potentially more than this and could include forgiveness of sin as well as physical recovery (*eg* the healing of the paralytic, Mark 2: 1-12). By His death on the Cross Jesus offered Himself as a once-for-all sacrifice for the forgiveness of sin and the restoration of human relationships (Romans 5: 6-11; Hebrews 7: 27, 10: 12-18). In this way, He provided the basis for a comprehensive ministry of healing available to all humankind.

"The pollution of our environment and the destruction of natural resources affects the health of humankind far more significantly than we realise."

The Need for Healing

Created healthy, human beings have not remained so. John Baillie said: "We cannot say that human nature is a good thing. Also we cannot say that it is a bad thing, nor a bad thing improving with time. It is a good thing spoiled."[3]

Human beings will be unhealthy if their **relation to their physical environment** is wrong. The creation story implies a continuity between humanity and nature, such that if this is disrupted the human being becomes unhealthy. Thus the healing ministry of the Church extends to ecological, indeed cosmological, dimensions. The pollution of our environment and the destruction of natural resources affects the health of humankind far more significantly than we realise.

Human beings will be unhealthy if their **relation to their social environment** is disrupted. There is a continuity of relationships between the individual and his/her fellow human beings, and the results of broken relationships at personal, community, national and international level creates havoc on our health. Perhaps this is most clearly seen in the unequal distribution of resources, *eg* medical care.

---

3   Divinity Class Lectures, 1946.

Part of the Church's healing ministry is to ensure that adequate distribution takes place, initially by its own use of its resources and by pressure on governments.

Human beings are unhealthy when there is the **disintegration of unity of a person's life**. Our loss of centre and identity is witnessed by the increasing results of anxiety, fear and guilt, namely emotional and nervous breakdown. These are not only signs of a sick person, but of a society which is in itself sick. The Church's healing ministry may here involve the extending of counselling and small-group therapy where persons, by being in communication with other persons, may rediscover their lost centre of being and regain a sense of personal integrity.

> "We cannot – nor can a doctor – ultimately uphold life, therefore we must turn and acknowledge our creaturely dependence on God."

Finally, we can say that our health is found in a **right relation with God**. We are mortal and finite, we face a death from which no experience of healing (which for us now is always fragmentary and contingent) can deliver us. We cannot – nor can a doctor – ultimately uphold life, therefore we must turn and acknowledge our creaturely dependence on God. Ultimately our personal integration, our communion with our fellow human beings and our stewardship of creation, depend on our being in relation to God. Health and salvation are at this point identical. Health in the ultimate sense of the word, health as identical with salvation, is life in faith and love. Healing under the impact of God's presence does not belittle or negate medicine, psychotherapy, political action – over social injustice or ecological protest; nor does the reverse happen. Rather, the healing impact of God integrates all of these necessary approaches to the different dimensions of healing.

The Healing Ministry

That the healing ministry of Jesus is intended to be continued by the Church is shown by the examples of healing by Paul and other Christian leaders, by the specific reference to a gift of healing (1 Corinthians 12: 7-11), and by a description of a procedure for the healing of the sick in the context of the congregation in James 5: 13-16. It is healing for the body as well as for mind and soul.

" ... in Christian practice the focus has been too often on the soul to the exclusion of the body."

The Church has not always captured the full flavour of the place given in the Bible to things of the body. A standard text book on theology published at the end of last century dismissed it as such: "As to the body of man, theology is not concerned with it, except to note how truly, both in material and structure, it is part of the physical universe."[4] But as Bonhoeffer has reminded us, God has ordained that there should be human life on earth only in the form of bodily life.[5] The body was the medium also for the Incarnation. Biblical teaching, also, is that at resurrection the form of our body will not be discarded, although it will be changed from a natural body to a spiritual one in the likeness of Christ (1 Corinthians 15: 42-49). In spite of this, in Christian practice the focus has been too often on the soul to the exclusion of the body.

The phrase "ministry of healing" first appeared in modern times as the title of a booklet written by the Rev. A J Gordon DD, a Baptist pastor from Boston, Massachusetts, and published in 1881.[6] Since then it has become the common term to describe the involvement of

---

4   W N Clarke: *An Outline of Christian Theology* (Edinburgh: T&T Clark, 1898), sixth edition, p 184.
5   Dietrich Bonhoeffer: *Ethics* (London: Collins/Fontana, 1964), p 156.
6   A J Gordon: *The Ministry of Healing* (London: Hodder & Stoughton, 1882).

the Church in what has been variously called faith-healing, divine healing, spiritual healing, charismatic healing and (by doctors) non-conventional therapy.

There are two senses in which the phrase "healing ministry" may be used. In the wider sense, it describes all activity which is directed to the healing and care of the sick. The human body and mind were created with self-healing properties; the healing of wounds and fractures are obvious examples, together with the action of the natural immune defence systems present in the tissues of the body. Surrounding us also in the created world are healing substances which may be used in the treatment of disease or injury, such as the group of antibiotic compounds derived from moulds. In this sense, all those concerned with health care in whatever capacity join in the ministry of healing, and God as Creator has provided within creation the means of our being healed.

> "Sometimes it is suggested that the Church's ministry of healing is an alternative to orthodox medical healing, and even in competition with it."

Another use of the term is in the more restricted sense of the ministry of Christian healing. It is the question of how God as redeemer and Holy Spirit provides the means of our being healed. Sometimes it is suggested that the Church's ministry of healing is an alternative to orthodox medical healing and even in competition with it. It is the growing interest in such patterns of personal healing, seen across the whole spectrum of the Church, that has prompted the renewed discussion to which this Report is a response, and which is developed more fully in the next section below.

We may summarise the scope of healing in the following propositions:

- healing extends to all aspects of human life and being and not only to the physical aspects;
- healing includes all effective methods of treatment and care whether these are by self-help, "orthodox" medicine or complementary therapies;

- healing, understood as the restoration to wholeness of a human being, is only part of the total approach to health and health care. It must be accompanied by measures which promote positive health and prevent disease and sickness.
- Healing never gives immunity against the causes of death and so is never complete in this life. Complete healing will only occur at the resurrection.

"Healing never gives immunity against the causes of death and so is never complete in this life."

Exercising the Healing Ministry

The Church becomes involved in healing ministry:

- because it is concerned for the well-being of human beings;
- because it believes that health in the fullest sense is the will of God for human beings;
- because it believes that all healing ultimately comes from God although it may be mediated through human agents;
- because the healing of all aspects of human life and being belongs to the gospel of Jesus Christ;
- because it has before it the example of Jesus Christ and the apostles;
- because it believes that it is the will of Christ that His disciples should heal the sick (Matthew 10: 8; Luke 10: 9);
- because the Second Great Commandment enjoins us to love our neighbour as ourselves;

- because the Church has a contribution to health and healing that no other agency can provide, namely the gospel of redemption and forgiveness through the grace of God without which we cannot be made truly whole (Romans 5: 10).

Rather than ask the question "How does the Church become involved in the healing ministry?", we should ask "How do its members come to realise that they are already involved in such a ministry?" This can only be by the Church clearly teaching that this is so: that every service of worship in which prayer is offered to God, in which His praise is sung, His Word read and expounded, and the Sacraments celebrated, is a healing service in which people may experience the healing and redeeming grace of God. Other special services of intercession for the sick or for the laying on of hands may be held, but they should not disguise this fact that the normal Sunday service may equally be a source of healing in which people may find shalom and forgiveness.

> "All Church members practise a healing ministry, through their daily work and witness, in their lifestyle."

There is still in the minds of many an assumption that healing in a Christian context necessarily and only means healing of a special kind exercised in a special way. For example, the methods of healing are usually those of prayer accompanied by the laying on of hands and sometimes anointing with oil. The Church, however, has traditionally emphasized the importance of comprehensive health care, not least in missionary contexts where hospitals have been built and professional care supplied. "Christian" healing is not an alternative to this but undergirds and complements it. "All healing is ultimately of God, who alone is the source of life and well-being. All those who combat and overcome disease are the agents God uses" (1958 Report).

All Church members practise a healing ministry, through their daily work and witness, in their lifestyle, and in their neighbourly concern for the health and healing of others. Some, however, play a special role: (a) those trained and experienced in medical, nursing and paramedical methods of healing, serving in Christian institutions, private health care, or in the National Health Service; (b) those trained in social work working in welfare agencies of the Church; (c) chaplains to various institutions, hospitals, prisons, industry; (d) ministers, the diaconate, readers who engage in pastoral ministry and in the leading of worship; (e) those who understand themselves to have received a special call to a ministry of Christian healing as a gift of the Holy Spirit.

> " ... today the function of the Christian congregation is to preach the gospel of redemption and forgiveness in order to lead people to faith in Him."

Developing the Healing Ministry

The Church encourages the development of the healing ministry:

- **by proclaiming the love of God for all people and His offer of redemption;**
- **by the promotion of a Christian lifestyle which leads to health in person and community;**
- **by encouraging members to seek professional training in health care;**
- **by supporting members who work in health care, in the social services, and in social action;**
- **by establishing patterns of care and facilities where these do not exist;**
- **by engaging in worship that takes seriously the needs of those**

who are gathered and by educating members in the healing dimension of worship; by providing the opportunity for special prayers for the sick together with the laying on of hands where appropriate;

- and by co-operating with other agencies where possible.

The base for all these activities is the congregation of Christian people. As Jesus sent out His disciples to preach, teach and heal, so today the function of the Christian congregation is to preach the gospel of redemption and forgiveness in order to lead people to faith in Him, to teach the people of God their

" ... the ministry of healing is potentially a part of any regular services of the Church, including Holy Communion."

Christian responsibilities and to provide healing for those who are sick or disabled in body, mind or spirit. In this way each congregation of God's people can be a therapeutic community in the fullest sense of that term.

RESOURCES for the HEALING MINISTRY

There are several forms and orders which have been prepared specifically for occasions when healing is the focus of worship. In *Common Order* (1994), for example, a form of intercessory prayer combined with an act of healing is provided. An introduction affirms that the ministry of healing is potentially a part of any of the regular services of the Church, including the service of Holy Communion. It acknowledges, however, that often a more informal atmosphere is desirable. In that context the importance of hearing the healing gospel, as well as shared or open intercession, is emphasised. The variety of ministrations and acts which are intended to convey the promise of healing in the Christian tradition is noted, and emphasis is placed on the need to find the forms most appropriate for local needs. Also offered are practical suggestions on making the most effective use of the material provided and of the occasions themselves.

There are several other forms which repay study, including the **United Reformed Church's Service of Healing (1991)**[7], the **Church of England's Liturgy for the Sick,**[8] the **Baptist Church's Services of Healing.**[9] A recent and most useful publication is *Guidelines for Good Practice*, **published for the Methodist Church and the Churches' Council for Health and Healing,**[10] which covers such matters as the importance of confidentiality, accountability, the role of non-verbal communication *etc*, as well as discussions of anointing and the laying on of hands, together with a "code of practice" for those engaged in healing ministry.

"The considerable variety of approach represented and of experience gained was seen to provide guidance for the development of such a ministry across a wide spectrum."

Having examined these resources, it was felt unnecessary to produce any further set of guidelines relating to the conduct of and approach to the ministry of healing. The considerable variety of approach represented and of experience gained was seen to provide guidance for the development of such a ministry across a wide spectrum. There is also already a range of books and other resources which will be found helpful to those who wish to widen and deepen their appreciation and understanding of the healing ministry. These are listed at the end of this Report.

---

7   86 Tavistock Place, London WC1H 9RT.
8   Grove Books, Bramcote, Notts NG9 3DS.
9   Baptist Union, 4 Southampton Row, London WC1B 4AB.
10 Methodist Publishing House, 20 Ivatt Way, Peterborough PE3 7PG.

A LETTER to SOMEONE
embarking on a HEALING MINISTRY

Dear Friend,

You ask about the healing ministry, what it is, what it would mean for you, and for others in the congregation, and you're wondering if you're being called to embark on it. My advice lies somewhere between our Lord's parable about sitting down to count the cost, and St Paul

> "A healing ministry should be theologically grounded and can be exercised only in love."

telling us "quench not the spirit". I will assume you have read the theological statement, and some of the books suggested, and are praying about it.

Martin Luther said: "The Holy Spirit alone makes true preachers. If He does not do it, it is not done." This would also be true of healing.

From a human point of view, a healing ministry is not to be strived after, only accepted, as a work of grace. It should not be separated from the preaching of the Word (being reconciled to God is the primary healing), nor from worship – praising God not only prepares people for healing, it can be healing in itself. Nor should it be separated from the fellowship of believers (it is a gift given to the Church).

None of us should be threatened if another member of the Body of Christ within our congregation is particularly gifted in this way. As with all gifts, however, it must be surrendered to God, otherwise we end up seeking glory for ourselves. A healing ministry should be theologically grounded, and can be exercised only in love. It is based on the example and command of our Lord, and depends entirely on His grace.

Pastoral care, including counsel, should be given before, during and following ministry. Read an appropriate scripture passage before praying with someone. We want to convey an expectancy without raising false expectations: healing can take time, and while we can hope for physical, mental and spiritual cure, our aim is wholeness, in body, mind and spirit – and holiness, a way of life that glorifies God.

> "A ministry of healing often requires us to simplify our faith, and revise theological positions."

It is wise not to act alone: support should be provided both for the person praying and the person being prayed for. Healing, like all ministry, is to be seen as an activity of the whole congregation – restoring broken relationships, establishing healthy communities, working for the healing of the nations, setting people free literally, metaphorically, emotionally and spiritually. Every member is involved in healing – through love and prayer – as every member is involved in mission – through love and prayer.

All ministry derives from, and is sustained by, prayer (*ie* an intimate living relationship with God), and this is especially true of a healing ministry. Therefore, learning about healing means simply learning to pray, sometimes over many years; and it means learning to love, and to have compassion. Guidelines for healing are not different in character from guidelines for all ministry – it is a calling, a gift, a burden, a privilege, a sacrifice, a joy; it includes serving and leading, teaching and caring. It means being used by God to bring blessing to others and being blessed in the process.

All of us are on a pilgrimage, a growing together in grace, where we are always learning from one another, and from Christ, who alone is the Great Physician. Prayers should be made continually for those in the medical and related professions – most of God's healing comes through them. Do not overlook how much healing would come to millions if we could but share our daily bread.

A ministry of healing often requires us to simplify our faith, and revise theological positions. It is essential that our lifestyle is consistent with our message, other-wise we are not credible: we remain all too human, wounded healers. Not infrequently people involved in this ministry have themselves an unhealed "thorn in the flesh".

> "The healing ministry will be controversial: it was so for Jesus."

There must be a sensitivity and humility, combined with strength and restraint, otherwise we will not be approached for healing and prayer. There needs to be a readiness to carry the burdens of others, to share their pain, sometimes confusion, and mutual disappointment. This is a ministry in which we are not in control. We make introductions, in prayer, and stand aside and let the Holy Spirit work. We learn to wait and to listen.

We want to learn when to defend and when not to defend the ministry of healing.

There is no "technique", nor order of service that "works". Our Lord treated everyone differently, personally, always with com-passion and grace. We do not find that our Lord always prayed with people: sometimes "He healed them all", sometimes only one person was healed and others weren't; sometimes touching, sometimes not; sometimes by His word, or by His friendship; sometimes in public, other times in private, sometimes never meeting the person.

The healing ministry will be controversial: it was so for Jesus. Some will oppose, rationally and irrationally; some will exaggerate, fascinated by the extraordinary. There is always a temptation to degenerate into the esoteric, or to seek kudos, or to think ourselves wiser or holier than in our hearts we know ourselves to be.

If you are sure you are being called to a ministry of healing, it helps if you can start alongside someone who is already practising. As with all learning:

1   I do it, you watch;
2   we do it together;
3   you do it, I watch.

Find that person of experience with whom you can talk freely, pray deeply, and refer to frequently.

There is, however, no way round the initial step of faith.

The Lord be with you.

FURTHER READING

Healing and the Church, John Wilkinson (Handsel Press).

Occasional Papers, Christian Fellowship and Healing (Eric Liddell Centre).

The Forgotten Talent, Cameron Peddie (Arthur James).

Healing, Frances McNutt (Ave Maria).

The Healing Light, Agnes Sanford (Arthur James).

The Question of Healing Services, John Richards (Renewal Servicing).

God Does Heal Today, Robert Dickinson (Paternoster Press).

Saints for Healing, Anglican Renewal Ministries, PO Box 366, Addlestone, Weybridge, Surrey KT15 3UL.

Power Healing, John Wimber (Hodder & Stoughton).

The Christian Healing Ministry, Morris Maddocks (SPCK).

Come Holy Spirit Come, David Pytches (Hodder & Stoughton).

The Bible and Healing, John Wilkinson (Handsel Press).

Health and Healing: A Ministry to Wholeness, Denis Duncan (Saint Andrew Press).

Creative Silence, Denis Duncan.

Prayers and Ideas for Healing Services, Ian Cowie (Wild Goose Publications).

General Assembly Reports 1955, 1958 and 1980 onwards, Board of Social Responsibility. [Copies of the 1955 and 1958 reports are available from the Board of Social Responsibility at Charis House, 47 Milton Road East, Edinburgh EH15 2SR.]

DISCUSSION QUESTIONS
on HEALTH and HEALING

BELOW are two sets of questions which we hope will stimulate discussion about health and healing, whether you are using them on your own, or in a group setting.

SET ONE

Health

- What do we mean by "health" in ordinary speech? Can you suggest other words which may be used to describe health?
- How do we know that we are healthy? What are the signs of health in a person?
- Has the Bible anything to say about "health"?
- Why is it important to agree on what we mean by "health"?

Healing

- What do we mean by "healing"?
- Why do we need to be healed?
- What is meant by "gifts of healing" mentioned by Paul three times in chapter 12 of his first letter to the Corinthians? See verses 9, 28 and 30 of this chapter.
- Is such a gift still available to individuals in the Church?
- If it is, how can we recognise that a person has a gift of healing?

Healing and the Church

- What has the Church to do with healing?
- What resources does the Church have which are important in healing?
- What special contribution can the Church make to healing?
- Should we expect miracles of healing in the life of the Church today similar to those described in the Bible?

The Ministry of Healing

- What do you understand this phrase to mean?
- Do you agree that the Church has a ministry of healing?
- Why should the Church become involved in the ministry of healing?
- How does the Church become involved?
- In what kind of healing should the Church be involved?
- What is the relationship of the Church's ministry of healing to the kind of healing practised by the health care professions?
- Has the Church any share in the practice of healing by the medical and other professions?
- How does the Church practise a ministry of healing?
- Who should practise the ministry of healing in the Church?
- What is meant by saying that the base for all the healing activities of the Church is the congregation?
- How does a congregation exercise its ministry of healing?

Healing Services

- Does the ministry of healing require special healing services?
- Does healing occur in "ordinary" services of worship?
- Does every congregation need to have special healing services?

- How may special healing services be introduced into the life of a congregation?
- What form should a special healing service take?
- Who should lead and take part in a healing service?
- What preparation is required for a healing service?
- Is follow-up to such a service important whether or not healing has occurred?
- What if healing does not occur?

SET TWO

- Can you think of where and when you experienced what the Bible describes as *shalom*?
- "In Christian practice the focus [of healing] has been too often in the soul, to the exclusion of the body." Do you agree?
- "Complete healing will only occur at the resurrection." Is this an excuse not to pray at all, or an excuse when physical healing does not follow prayer?
- All church members practise a healing ministry, through their daily work and witness, in their lifestyle, and in their neighbourly concern for the healing of others. To what extent is this true? To what extent is it true of you?
- "Each congregation is a therapeutic community."
  "The Church is God's healing agency on earth."
  Are these definitions accurate/challenging/exciting?
- In what ways was our Lord's healing ministry controversial?
- What were some of the reactions when he healed people?
- J McManus said, "Preaching without healing is powerless, healing without preaching is pointless." Is he right?
- In what way do you need to be healed – in body, in mind, in your relationships, in spirit … ?
- What gifts of the Spirit do we individually and as a Church need in order to do all God asks us to do?

- List some of the ways God is already using the Church to bring healing to people.
- Do all forms of healing on offer today bring glory to God?
- Why do you think healing has been described as the Church's "forgotten talent"? How can we recover this gift, and command?
- "Preach the gospel, heal the sick." Do you think this command was "time-limited", meant only for first century Christians?
- "Christians are wounded healers." Do you agree?
- "The kingdom of God is creation healed" (H Kung). Discuss.
- Who taught you to pray?
- Give instance of different types of healing
  - (a) in the Bible
  - (b) nowadays.
- If we can pray about anything, why can we not pray for healing? Discuss.

THE FUTURE OF THE FAMILY
A Crisis of Commitment
More people than ever are divorcing, bringing up children alone or living as a couple without marrying. So is family life important? Is any action needed to support it? These and other questions are tackled from a Christian perspective.
Paper/0 86153 157 4/70pp/£3.95

HUMAN GENETICS
A Christian Perspective
Human Genetics affects us all. It is changing the way we all look at human life, and understand ourselves. Many people look Church for guidance and support. This book offers everyone an informed starting point for further reflection from a Christian perspective.
Paper/0 86153 208 2/76pp/£4.95

PRE-CONCEIVED IDEAS
A Christian Perspective of IVF and Embryology
Many people have pre-conceived ideas about fertilisation and embryology. The Church of Scotland gives a Christian perspective on these complex issues, offering helpful advice about possibilities and problems of starting a family by IVF and other methods.
Paper/0 86153 223 6/96pp/£5.95

EUTHANASIA
A Christian Perspective
Euthanasia is an emotional and complex subject. The moral and ethical issues raise difficult questions for all those involved in the care of a terminally ill person. This book tackles some of the common questions about euthanasia from a Christian perspective and gives sound answers.
Paper/0 86153 252 X/72pp/£4.95

Marriage PLUS
A Study Pack for Couples
A pack for couples about to get married, or for use by those leading marriage preparation classes.
£4.00

HIV/AIDS
Resource Pack
A helpful pack divided into sections, including worship, bible readings and a contact list.
£4.00

Young People and the Media
Study Pack
Ideal discussion starter split into six main sections, with relevant questions and bible readings.
£2.50

Good News for a Change
A joint publication between the Boards of Social Responsibility, National Mission and World Mission, which tells good news stories from congregations in Scotland and overseas.
Paper/0 86153 257 0/44pp/£3.50

Good News for a Change and the books on page 26 are available from SAINT ANDREW PRESS
Church of Scotland, 121 George Street,
Edinburgh EH2 4YN
and from all good bookshops.

The packs (above) are available direct from
CHURCH of SCOTLAND
BOARD of SOCIAL RESPONSIBILITY
Charis House, 47 Milton Road East,
Edinburgh EH15 2SR.

(Add £1.00 p&p for each item ordered.
Cheques payable to 'Board of Social Responsibility'.)

The CHURCH of SCOTLAND
BOARD of SOCIAL RESPONSIBILITY

THANK you for buying this book. We hope you found it helpful. If you would like to comment on its contents please write to our Public Relations Officer, Hugh Brown, at Charis House (address below).

The Church of Scotland Board of Social Responsibility is one of the largest providers of social care in Scotland. It employs around 1600 people in 90 homes, units and projects across Scotland from Shetland to Dumfries. It cares for over 4000 people in need every day of the year. Although staff have a Christian commitment, the Board's services are offered to those of all faiths or none. Our Mission Statement is:

"In Christ's name we seek to retain and regain the highest quality of life which each individual is capable of experiencing at any given time."

As well as being the Church of Scotland's social work department, the Board also guides the Church on social, moral and ethical issues affecting society. The books mentioned on the previous pages have been produced after relevant reports were accepted by the General Assembly of the Church of Scotland.

The Board relies on funding from a number of sources to continue its work in Scotland with people who need care, support and help. An important contribution comes from donations, gift aid and legacies. If you would like to become a supporter of the Board, or perhaps find out more about contributing financially, please contact our Fundraising Officer, Maurice Houston, at Charis House, 47 Milton Road East, Edinburgh EH15 2SR (Tel: 0131 657 2000; Fax: 0131 657 5000; E-mail: info@charis.org.uk).